VAMPIRE
hunter's Guide

Otto De'Ath

LONDON•SYDNEY

Ever wandered down a dark shortcut, only to regret it halfway? Odd shapes and mysterious sounds lurk in the dark: what could they be? Probably just an old rubbish bin in a bush, or the wind flapping a plastic bag in a tree. Or maybe... a horde of vampires, ready to leap out and drain your blood!

If it IS a vampire horde waiting for you on your way home, what do you do? This book tells you everything you need to know: how to recognise vampires, ways of escaping them, and even how to destroy one.

Good luck!

Otto De'ath

CONTENTS

Words in bold are in the glossary.

Vampires everywhere!

Make no mistake – vampires are everywhere! For hundreds of years, these creatures have hidden in the shadows, emerging at night to feed on blood.

Vampires – the Undead

Vampires survive by drinking the blood of a living human. Eventually, the human runs out of blood and dies. Then they too become a vampire. Their body rises in darkness and seeks out humans to feast upon. Vampires are sometimes called the Undead. Being dead already, they can be tricky to destroy.

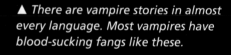

▲ There are vampire stories in almost every language. Most vampires have blood-sucking fangs like these.

Vampire hunters

Vampire hunters are a vampire's deadliest enemy. They know everything about the bloodsucking beasts: their hang-outs, the forms they take, their habits, skills, weapons and weaknesses. But most important of all, vampire hunters know how to destroy these undead creatures.

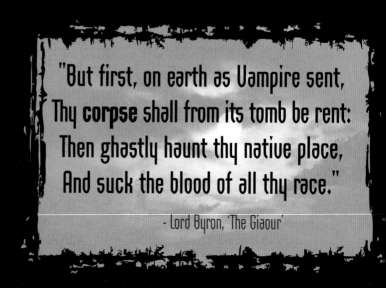

"But first, on earth as Vampire sent,
Thy **corpse** shall from its tomb be rent:
Then ghastly haunt thy native place,
And suck the blood of all thy race."

- Lord Byron, 'The Giaour'

Becoming a vampire hunter

This book is your first step to becoming a vampire hunter. It is filled with case studies of vampires from around the world. You will learn about:

- The different forms in which vampires appear.
- The deadly powers of the vampire.
- How vampires work with human **allies.**
- How to fight and destroy vampires.

Are you ready to join the battle against them?

▼ Films such as Twilight can make vampires look attractive. But there is nothing lovely about them!

Holy Water

twilight
IN THEATRES
12·12·08
TWILIGHTTHEMOVIE.COM

Vampire Hunter's Kit

Vampire hunters have several weapons They include:

- Garlic – it stops vampires from crossing a **threshold.**

- A cross – vampires shrink away from them.

- Holy water (water blessed by a priest) – it burns vampires.

- A wooden stake – it can be driven through a vampire's heart to destroy it.

Generations of vampire hunters have perfected their skills in the Carpathian Mountains in Central Europe. For centuries, people there have lived in fear of the vampire menace.

◀ *Carpathian vampires often visit their victims while they are peacefully asleep.*

▼ *The Carpathian Mountains are found in the heart of Europe.*

Vampire abilities

Carpathian vampires have many special, supernatural powers. A vampire hunter needs to remember them all. Otherwise, the hunter can become the hunted!

• In the night, vampires can shape-shift – they change their shape to become, for example, a bat, wolf or giant dog, or even a cloud of mist.

• Vampires can pass through the tiniest cracks, such as the gap under a door.

• They have the strength of ten men.

• The oldest, most powerful vampires are able to exert a **hypnotic** power over their victims.

Limits on a vampire's powers

With all these powers it might seem that Carpathian vampires are invincible. Not so! They have fatal weaknesses, which a vampire hunter can use to his or her advantage:

- Some vampires are destroyed if they are caught in the sunlight.
- During the day, vampires must rest in their home soil, usually in a coffin or case of some kind. They enter a kind of sleep, during which they are powerless.
- Vampires can only enter a building if they have been invited.
- They cannot pass running water except at high or low tide.

Vampire Names

In Central Europe, vampires are known by many different names:

- strigoi in Romania
- upierczi in Russia and Poland
- tenatz in Montenegro
- obur in Bulgaria.

▼ For hundreds of years, villagers in the vampire heartland have bolted their doors at night for fear of vampires.

WARDING OFF THE EVIL EYE

If you see people in the Carpathians pointing two fingers at someone's face, watch out! They are making a gesture to ward off the 'Evil Eye'. This is bad luck caused by contact with beings such as vampires or witches.

Dracula!

Imagine yourself travelling alone, crossing a high pass of the Transylvanian mountains in Romania. As night falls, you spot a castle. A light glows in a window. Is this a place to seek shelter?

No! Inside lives the father of all vampires. A vampire so powerful that only a team of crack vampire hunters would have a chance against him. This is the home of the most famous Carpathian vampire of all – Count Dracula.

Characteristics and behaviour

As a man, Dracula was a great leader, a member of a secret society called the Order of the Dragon. He somehow learnt the magic to transform himself into the first vampire.

◄ Castle Bran in Transylvania, where Dracula is believed to live.

Vampire Fact File

Name: Count Dracula
Location: Transylvania
Age: 550 years

Combat and destruction

Dracula is extremely powerful and very cunning. But in theory, he can be caught in the same ways as any other Carpathian vampire:

- Garlic around a doorway or across a threshold forms a barrier vampires cannot cross.
- Placing the branch of a wild rose in their coffin makes it impossible for a vampire to leave it.
- Holy water burns vampires, and they are scared of crosses.
- Vampires can be killed by a silver bullet, a stake through the heart or by cutting off their head and stuffing their mouth full of garlic.

"As the Count leaned over me and his hands touched me... a horrible feeling of nausea came over me, which, do what I would, I could not conceal."

– From Bram Stoker's novel *Dracula*

▼ Dracula's legend has spread so far that his character has featured in hundreds of Hollywood movies.

VAMPIRE I.Q. TEST!

A sure test for suspected vampires is that their reflection cannot be seen in a mirror.

The vampires of Haidamak

On a dark, cold night in the Hungarian town of Haidamak, an old man walked into a house and sat beside the owner during dinner. The dinner guests were terrified. The old man was the owner's father – who had been dead for ten years!

Everyone knew what the old man wanted: he had come to take his son away. And sure enough, the next morning his son was found dead in his bed.

▲ *The old man drank his son's blood while he slept.*

Vampire Fact File

Name: Not known
Location: Haidamak, Hungary
Age: Nearly 300 years

Expedition to the graveyard

A local man called Count Cabreras decided to investigate. He ordered his soldiers to dig up the old man's coffin and open it. Despite being dead for ten years, the old man looked alive! The Count cut off the old man's head, and immediately a **torrent** of blood poured out.

▲ *The Count and his men were greeted by a gruesome discovery when they opened the old man's coffin.*

Further vampires are discovered

The Count and his soldiers soon discovered that there were more vampires in the village:

- The first was a man who had been dead for 30 years, but whose body was perfectly preserved. The soldiers dug him up, and drove an iron nail through his head.
- The second vampire had died 16 years before, but again was perfectly preserved. This time the Count ordered his men to burn the body.

"These vampires were corpses, who went out of their graves at night to suck the blood of the living, either at their throats or stomachs... the sucking corpses grew fat, got rosy, and enjoyed an excellent appetite."

– an early report of vampires from the French writer Voltaire.

The vrykolakas

✝ of

Greece

Imagine yourself in a house in a Greek mountain village. In the darkness outside, the wind howls. Suddenly, there is a loud knock on the door, and a voice calls the owner's name. Perhaps it is a vampire or a vrykolakas.

If the vrykolakas does not hear a reply, it will pass on to another house. But anyone who opens the door is cursed. Within days

▲ Vampire hunters disagree about whether a vrykolakas is a vampire, werewolf, or cross between the two. Whatever it is, never open the door to one!

Vampire Fact File

Name: Vrykolakas
Location: most common in Greece
Age: at least 450 years

they too will become a vrykolakas. That's why people in some Greek villages never answer the door the first time you knock!

Characteristics and behaviour

Some people say vrykolakas are the bodies of those who have lived an unholy life. Their bodies do not rot, and they have red eyes, fangs and hairy hands.

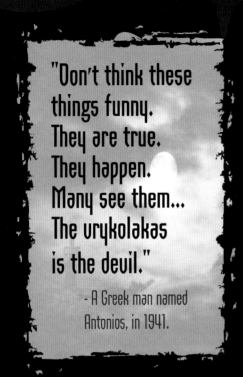

"Don't think these things funny. They are true. They happen. Many see them... The vrykolakas is the devil."

— A Greek man named Antonios, in 1941.

Detection and destruction

Clues that a vrykolakas is in the area include: diseases spreading, people being crushed or suffocated to death in their sleep, and mysterious accidents occurring.

The vrykolakas can only be destroyed in its grave. Some say that it only rests there on a Saturday. There are a few ways to destroy the vrykolakas, depending on what tools are available:

• Beheading it with a sword or large dagger,
• Impaling it with a wooden stake,
• Cutting it into pieces,
• Burning it.

◄ Once a vrykolakas is inside a house, it will wreak deadly havoc. No one is likely to survive the night.

REDHEADS WATCH OUT!

At one time, the Greeks thought that all people with red hair and blue eyes were vrykolakas.

The case of Peter Plogojowitz

The case of Peter Plogojowitz is a chilling example of what can happen when vampires are let loose. Plogojowitz died aged 62 in 1725 in a village in Eastern Europe. Ten weeks later, the vampire Plogojowitz's reign of terror began.

Vampire Fact File

Name: Peter Plogojowitz
Location: Kisilova, Serbia
Age: died 1725

▲ This scene from a movie shows the villagers storming the home of the local governor, demanding that Plogojowitz's coffin be dug up.

The dead man reappears

First, villagers began to see Plogojowitz at night outside or beside their beds. He began to attack people: within 24 hours, they were dead. Next, Plogojowitz visited his son, demanding to be fed. When Plogojowitz was told to leave, he went crazy, and killed his son.

Nine people had now died at Plogojowitz's hands in a week. The villagers decided to take the law into their own hands. Armed with weapons, they went to the village priest and the local governor, and told them that Plogojowitz had to be dug up.

A terrible discovery

Plogojowitz's coffin was dug up.
When the villagers opened it,
a startling sight met their eyes.
Despite having died 11 weeks earlier,
Plogojowitz still looked completely
fresh. His skin had flaked off, but
new skin was growing underneath.
His nails were long, and fresh blood
dripped from his mouth.

The villagers were now certain that
Plogojowitz was a vampire, and drove
a wooden stake through his heart.
The local governor reported that the
body showed 'wild signs', with blood
spurting from the wound, before
coming to rest.

SCIENCE EXPLAINS?

Scientists now say that
by growing new skin,
nails and hair, Peter
Plogojowitz's dead body
was only behaving as
many (non-vampire)
corpses do. But of
course, that's exactly
what vampires would
WANT you to think…

▼ *Peter Plogojowitz was
killed for good when the
villagers buried a wooden
stake in his heart.*

Penanggalan of ✝ Malaysia

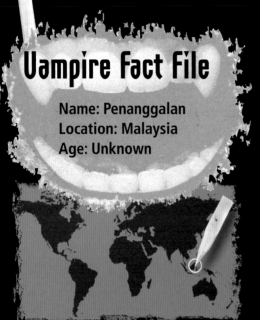

Vampire Fact File

Name: Penanggalan
Location: Malaysia
Age: Unknown

In Malaysia, there was once a plain woman who wanted to be beautiful. This woman knew black magic. She cast a spell, and the next day she was as beautiful as she had always dreamed.

The spell had a terrible price. Every night, the woman had to detach her head from her body, and fly through the skies, trailing her **entrails** behind her. She was searching for blood because only fresh blood could keep the spell working. She had become the first penanggalan.

Characteristics and behaviour

Penanggalan look like ordinary women during the day, but at night they transform. When she finds a victim, a penanggalan sucks out their blood using her long, fang-like teeth.

◀ *Penanggalan are always women and are extremely bloodthirsty.*

Detection

Tracking down a penanggalan's **lair** is not easy. The best way is to follow her back to where she has left her body. The next night, you will be able to go there while her head is away, and destroy the body. Another clue is that she will have a jar of vinegar on a shelf. This is used to shrink her insides down, and make them fit easily back inside her body.

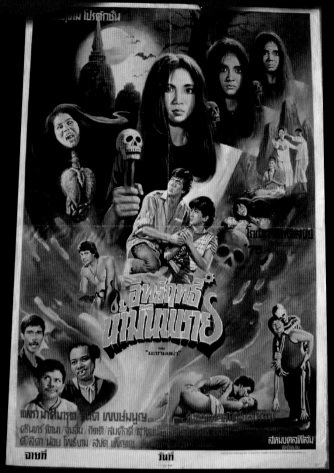

◀ *Malaysian horror films often feature penanggalan. In this poster there is one in the top left.*

Penanggalan v. Manananggal

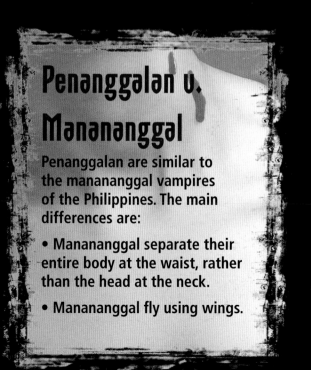

Penanggalan are similar to the manananggal vampires of the Philippines. The main differences are:

• Manananggal separate their entire body at the waist, rather than the head at the neck.

• Manananggal fly using wings.

Combat and destruction

There are several methods for fighting and destroying a penanggalan:

• To kill a penanggalan, you must attack her body while she is away. Some vampire hunters pour broken glass inside, which slices her entrails when she puts them back inside her body.

• Other vampire hunters sprinkle salt, garlic or ash into the body, or simply burn it.

Rokurokubi of Japan

If you are travelling through Japan on your hunt for vampires, take great care where you spend the night. You may be amongst bloodsucking, flesh-eating vampires called rokurokubi.

These vampires can be male or female. During the day, rokurokubi appear to be ordinary humans. It is only at night that they are able to stretch their necks huge distances, snaking round corners, through tiny windows, and over high walls. This makes it easy for them to get at victims who sleep thinking that they are safe from harm.

▶ Rokurokubi look just like normal people, apart from their extraordinarily long necks.

Vampire Fact File

Name: Rokurokubi
Location: Japan
Age: At least 2,000 years

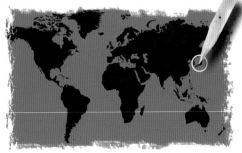

Characteristics and behaviour

Not all rokurokubi are vampires. Some are harmless **tricksters**, who love playing pranks on people. A few don't even KNOW they are rokurokubi. The vampire rokurokubi are humans punished for having lived an evil life. They drink the blood, or sometimes even eat the flesh, of humans. Their faces sometimes transform into those of oni – terrifying Japanese ogres.

▼ *A Japanese oni devil mask. Rokurokubi can sometimes take on the face of an oni.*

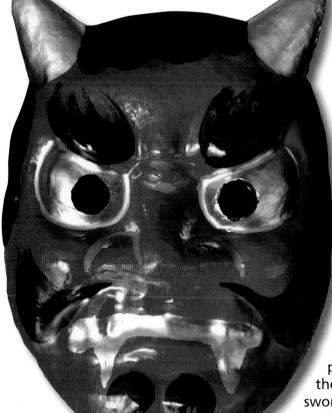

JAPANESE YÕKAI

Rokurokubi are just one kind of Japanese yōkai – supernatural creatures:
• Shape-shifting animals such as fox-like kitsune.
• Tsukumogami, household objects that come alive when they are 100 years old.
• Ohaguru-bettari, women with an extra, hungry mouth at the back of their head.

Detection and destruction

Rokurokubi may try to entice travellers to stay the night. If you suspect your hosts are rokurokubi, pretend to be asleep, but keep a careful watch. As soon as their neck stretches towards you, take action.

Reciting Buddhist prayers will stop a rokurokubi coming near you. Rokurokubi can be destroyed in the same ways as any other living creature. The most popular way is to cut off the rokurokubi's head with a sword or dagger while its neck is stretched out.

The loogaroo of the Caribbean

Vampire Fact File

Name: Loogaroo
Location: Haiti and other Caribbean islands; Louisiana, USA
Age: First reported 1700s

If you find yourself wandering the paths of a Caribbean island at night, be on your guard for a fiery ball of light making its way through the trees. It's a sure sign that a loogaroo is on the prowl.

The loogaroo is a female vampire, a witch or sorceress who has made a pact with the Devil. In return for supernatural powers, she must bring the Devil blood.

Characteristics and behaviour

When she's out looking for victims, the loogaroo leaves her skin behind. She hangs it from a silk-cotton tree, and heads off as a ball of fiery light.

Beware of a bright light that suddenly appears in the midst of some trees. It could mean a loogaroo is close!

Detection

In the daytime, loogaroos have a human form, and are tricky to spot. Dogs hate them, and will bark madly if a loogaroo comes near. If you wake in the morning feeling weak and more tired than when you went to bed, there may be a loogaroo around.

▲ *Caribbean vampires are closely associated with the voodoo religion. Here a woman in Haiti is under a voodoo spell.*

"The loogaroo is particularly obnoxious to dogs, and any person at whom apparently without cause dogs will bark furiously... is accounted infected with the vampire taint."

– From Montague Summers' *The Vampire, His Kith and Kin*, 1928.

Combat and destruction

If you do come across a loogaroo, the best ways to destroy one are:

- Scatter rice or sand in its path. The vampire will stop to count the grains, and can be caught and killed by the dawn.
- If you can find the loogaroo's skin, pound it to pieces mixed in with salt (below) and pepper. This makes it impossible for the loogaroo to return to her skin at dawn.

The Boo Hag of South Carolina

In the hot, steamy coastal lands of South Carolina and Georgia, USA, live the **Gullah** people. Their stories tell of a vampire that sucks the life out of you through your breath. This is the Boo Hag.

A Boo Hag doesn't always kill its victims. Often it leaves them a little breath, so that they can recover – and provide the Boo Hag with another meal later on. But if the Boo Hag likes the look of your skin, watch out! She doesn't have one of her own, and she might just take yours.

◄ *Boo Hag vampires are always red because they don't have a skin of their own.*

Characteristics and behaviour

In the daytime, Boo Hags look just like ordinary women. But at night they **slough** off their human skin, revealing the red-fleshed monster beneath. Then Boo Hags fly through the night air, looking for victims.

If you are feeling breathless and tired, it might be because the Boo Hag has been visiting you. Look out for a Boo Hag's skin hanging in your wardrobe at night.

Combat an

• You can kee
from a Boo H
broom beside
Hag will start
straws in it, a
by dawn, will

• To destroy a
must fill her s
pepper. Whe
it, her skin wi
crush her or e

DON'T LET dE BOO HAG RIDE YA

"I done been out and had my fun, but now
back, and my work's all done. So let me in
skin, for the Sun's about to crest, you kno
I'm a Boo Hag, and I needs my rest."

– The Boo Hag's rhyme

Scotland's Baobhan sith

Travelling through the Scottish Highlands at night can be lonely. ...d clings to your feet and ...eems that you will never ...ch home. But beware ...beautiful women who ...ddenly appear.

...hese women (many of whose ...ctims are handsome young men) ...e really Baobhan sith. They are ...il **faeries** – and all they want is ...ur blood.

...aracteristics
... behaviour

...he Baobhan sith use their beauty ... entice lonely travellers to join ...em around a fire. Then, using ...erie magic, they dance with the ...aveller until he falls asleep. Then the ...obhan sith pounce! Slicing open an **artery** with their long, ...arp fingernails, they drain their victim of blood.

▲ *The Baobhan sith are known to captivate lonely travellers.*

Vampire Fact File

Name: Baobhan sith
(pronounced Bavan Shee)
Location: Scotland
Age: Not known

If a beautiful woman on a lonely road asks you to dance round a fire with her, that'll be a BIG clue that you've met a Baobhan sith. Also, Baobhan sith can speak any language, but they always have a strange accent.

Combat and destruction

Like all faerie creatures, Baobhan sith can be harmed or even killed using iron. Being on horseback keeps you safe, because the creatures are afraid of the horse's iron shoes. Iron weapons, including nails, can also defeat them. If you keep the Baobhan sith occupied until dawn, it will disappear as the Sun rises.

BEWARE THE CELTIC LADIES!

The Baobhan sith are similar to other supernatural females in **Celtic** countries:

• **The beautiful Leanan sidhe in Ireland and the Isle of Man.**

• **The blood-sucking Dearg-due from Ireland.**

▲ *Baobhan sith can transform themselves into different creatures, including wolves.*

Australia's Yara-ma-yha-who

In the heat of Australia, it can be tempting to sit down under a tree to cool down. But be careful which tree you choose. Pick the wrong one, and you might find yourself face to face with Yara-ma-yha-who – the Australian vampire.

Yara-ma-yha-who waits in the branches of his tree for an unsuspecting victim. As they pass by or stop, he falls down on them. This is an odd vampire, for he has no teeth. Instead, he drains his victims using his sucker-like fingers and toes.

Vampire Fact File

Name: Yara-ma-yha-who
Location: Australia
Age: Not known

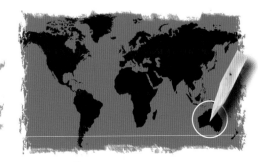

26

Characteristics and behaviour

Yara-ma-yha-who is about 1.2 metres tall, and red, with a large head. Once he has caught a victim, Yara-ma-yha-who sucks out nearly all their blood, leaving just enough to keep them alive. Then he goes off for a walk.

When he comes back, instead of sucking more blood, Yara-ma-yha-who swallows the victim whole – then vomits him or her back up again. This process goes on and on. Each time the victim gets smaller and smaller, and more and more like the Yara-ma-yha-who. Eventually, the victim becomes another Yara-ma-yha-who.

Escaping Yara-ma-yha-who

Yara-ma-yha-who is not a very good runner: if you can run off, he may not be able to catch you. Once in his clutches, there is only one chance of escape:

• When Yara-ma-yha-who vomits you back up the first time, he will tickle you to make sure you are still alive. Play dead.

• Yara-ma-yha-who will wander off and hide, watching to see if you are REALLY dead. Keep playing dead.

• Eventually, Yara-ma-yha-who will fall asleep. Run away – and keep running, as fast as you can.

WATCH OUT FOR FIGS!

Yara-ma-yha-who's favourite tree is a fig tree. He lives in the top branches – but comes down to the lower branches if he hears a possible victim approaching.

◀ Yara-ma-yha-who uses the suckers on his fingers to suck the blood from his victims.

Brahmaparusha † of India

Vampire Fact File

Name: Brahmaparusha
Location: Northern India
Age: over 2,000 years

▲ *Brahmaparusha attacks one of his unlucky victims.*

Vampire hunters have the courage and skills to survive in situations where others would perish. But there is one vampire that cannot be defeated. This vampire is an Indian demon called Brahmaparusha.

Brahmaparusha has a thirst for blood unlike any other vampire's. It can devour one, two, three or more people at a time. And it isn't satisfied with draining its victims of blood. Brahmaparusha also has a taste for brains.

Characteristics and behaviour

When Brahmaparusha catches a victim, he starts draining their blood. He carries a mug made from a human skull, which he uses for drinking the blood. Once the victim is drained, he lops off the top of their head and eats their brain like a boiled egg.

Detection and destruction

This is really not a hard vampire to spot: he will be wearing a necklace of human intestines, and possibly a crown made of more intestines. In addition, Brahmaparusha will have at least one human skull hanging from his belt.

Normally, there is more than one way to destroy a vampire. Unfortunately, there are NO ways to destroy Brahmaparusha. If he happens to be dancing when you meet him, you might just have a chance to get away: he only performs his ritual dance when he's full. Otherwise, say your prayers.

▲ *A baital is another kind of Indian vampire (see box right). It is half-bat and has powerful leathery wings.*

INDIAN VAMPIRES

Brahmaparusha is not the only type of vampire found in South Asia:

• In Sri Lanka, the rakshasa is a flesh-eating, blood-drinking horror.

• The churel is a black-tongued devourer of young men's life force.

• The baital is half-man, half-bat, and 1.5 metres tall.

Technical information

Words from this book:

allies
friends

artery
major blood vessel, carrying fresh blood from the heart

Celtic
where Celtic languages were once spoken: for example, Scotland, Ireland, Wales and parts of north-western France

corpse
dead body

entrails
internal (inside) parts of a body

Evil Eye
bad luck (or worse), caused by contact with beings that have supernatural powers – such as vampires or witches

faeries
supernatural beings

Gullah
African Americans who are descended from people brought to the USA over 300 years ago to work as slaves

hypnotic
using special techniques to control someone else's actions

lair
hide-out

nausea
feeling sick

slough
remove by sliding out of, like a snake out of its skin

threshold
line or doorway between one space and another

torrent
flow of a large amount of liquid.

trickster
mischievous being who likes to play practical jokes

Equipment

Always buy the best vampire-hunting equipment you can afford.

Crucifixes and crosses – size is not important. Vampires from Catholic countries may be more scared of crucifixes as they include a representation of Jesus's body on the cross, but either should work.

Garlic – freshly cut garlic leaves and bulbs are best, but older bulbs can be smeared around to leave their juice behind.

Holy water – do get your holy water from an approved source. There's nothing worse than throwing what you thought was holy water over a vampire, only to discover that it's actually flat lemonade.

Silver bullets – must be of high-grade silver. Vampires just spit out the low-grade stuff.

Stakes – the best stakes are very sharp at one end, and are about 45cm long. Flatten the other end so that it's easy to give it a good whack with the hammer.

More vampire information

Other books

A Practical Guide To Vampires
Lisa Trutkoff Trumbauer (Wizards of the Coast, 2009)
Information on a variety of vampires, their characters, physical appearance and weaknesses.

Informania: Vampires
Martin Jenkins (Walker Books, 2000)
Information on the stories of human vampires, their animal equivalents, and a list of some of the great vampire movies – plus a picture-story version of a novel about Dracula.

Vampires and Other Monstrous Creatures Julius Pemberton-Smythe (Harper Collins, 2008)
Roughly half this book is concerned with vampires, the rest with other supernatural creatures. The vampire sections give information about vampire origins, different types of vampire, and how to deal with them.

Although the following is an adult title, it would be useful to confident readers who want to find out more:

The Vampire Book: The Encyclopedia of the Undead J Gordon Melton (Visible Ink Press, 1994)

The Internet

www.monstropedia.org
This is a great, big rambling site, which is absolutely full of information about all kinds of weird, supernatural and scary creatures. To get to the vampire section, click on 'Corporeal undead', then 'Vampires'.

www.vampires.com
Definitely a site for teenagers, vampires.com allows you to keep up with vampires in the movies, TV, books and other popular culture.

Movies and DVDs

The Lost Boys
(1987, dir. Joel Schumacher)
One of the all-time great vampire movies. A family moves to a new town, only to discover that the pretty seaside resort is not quite as it seems in the tourist brochures.

Bram Stoker's Dracula
(1992, dir. Francis Ford Coppola)
A modern retelling of the original vampire story, written by the author Bram Stoker in 1897. An ancient vampire comes to England: can he be repelled before he becomes too powerful to defeat?

Dracula
(1931, dir. Tod Browning)
Worth seeing because this is a) the first-ever Dracula movie and b) it features Bela Lugosi as the best Dracula ever.

Note to parents and teachers: every effort has been made by the Publishers to ensure that these websites are suitable for children, that they are of the highest educational value, and that they contain no inappropriate or offensive material. However, because of the nature of the Internet, it is impossible to guarantee that the contents of these sites will not be altered. We strongly advise that Internet access is supervised by a responsible adult.

Index

First published in 2012 by
Franklin Watts
338 Euston Road
London NW1 3BH

Franklin Watts Australia
Level 17/207 Kent Street
Sydney NSW 2000

Copyright © Franklin Watts 2011

Series editors: Adrian Cole and Julia Bird
Art director: Jonathan Hair
Design: Mayer Media
Picture research: Diana Morris

A CIP catalogue record for this book
is available from the British Library.

Dewey number: 363.2

ISBN: 978 1 4451 0123 1

Printed in China

Franklin Watts is a division of
Hachette Children's Books,
an Hachette UK company.
www.hachette.co.uk

Acknowledgements:
Andreiuc88/Fotolia: 20b. Art Archive/Picture Desk: 29bl.
Thony Belizaire/Getty Images: 21t. Bettmann/Corbis: 15b.
Bliznetsov/Shutterstock: 7t, 17b, 29br. Caro/Bastien/Topfoto:
7b. Jackie Carvey/Shutterstock: 2. Shona Cowart/www.
laladexpress.com: 23c. Dinodia: 28c. Mary Evans PL: 24tr.
Mary Evans PL/Alamy: 10c. First Light/Alamy: 25b.
Fortean PL/Topfoto: 6t. Fotosutra/Shutterstock: 4b, 9t, 11b,
13t, 21bl, 23b. Gargonia/Shutterstock: 8b. The Granger
Collection/Topfoto: 9br. Peter Horree/Alamy: 22b.
Jitalia/istockphoto: 5ccr, 30cr. Renee Keith/istockphoto: 13bl.
André Klaassen/Shutterstock: 9bl, 13br, 15t, 19t, 25t, 27br.
Kurt Komoda/Getty Images: 16b, 27bl. Natalia Lukiyanova/
frenta/Shutterstock: 3. Maxxstudio/Shutterstock: 2-3, 30-31,
32. James McQuillan/istockphoto: 4tl, 5cl, 5ccl, 5cr, 8tl, 20t,
24tl, 28tl, 30l, 30tr. Monkey Business/Shutterstock: 21br.
Panyathai: 17t. Perrush/Shutterstock: front cover. Photos12/
Alamy: 1, 12t. Margaret M Stewart/Shutterstock: 4c.
© 2008 Summit Entertainment Inc. All Rights Reserved: 5t.
Collection Kharbine-Tapabor, Paris, France/Bridgeman Art
Library: 11t. 3drendering/Shutterstock: 5c. Universal/Kobal
Collection: 14b. Hideki Yoshihara/Aflo/Getty Images: 19b.
Austen Zaleski: 26t.